ISIS

GODDESS OF LOVE, HEALING, AND MAGIC

Isis: Goddess of Love, Healing, and Magic

Copyright © Nichole Muir Goddess Wisdom

www.nicholemuir.com

All right reserved. No part of this book may be reproduced by any mechanical, photographic, or electronic process, or in the form of a phonographic recording: nor may it be stored in a retrieval system, transmitted, or otherwise be copied for public or private use- other than for "fair use" as brief quotation embodied in articles and reviews – without prior written permission of the publisher

Please note the information contained within this document is for educational and entertainment purposes only. All effort has been executed to present accurate, up to date, and reliable, complete information. No warranties of any kind are declared or implied.

Readers acknowledge that the author is not engaging in the rendering of legal, financial, medical or professional advice. The content within this book has been derived from various sources. Please consult a licensed professional before attempting any techniques outlined in this book.

Contents

Chapter 1: The Enigma of Isis 4

Chapter 2: Isis and Osiris: A Tale of Love 10

Chapter 3: The Magical Powers of Isis 16

Chapter 4: Isis as a Healing Goddess 22

Chapter 5: Isis in the Everyday Life of Ancient Egypt 28

Chapter 6: Symbols of Isis 34

Chapter 7: Isis and the Afterlife 39

Chapter 8: The Priesthood of Isis 44

Chapter 9: The Spread of Isis's Cult 49

Chapter 10: Isis in Modern Spirituality 54

Chapter 11: Isis and Her Siblings 59

Chapter 12: The Festivals of Isis 64

Chapter 13: Isis in Art and Iconography 69

Chapter 14: The Protective Goddess 74

Chapter 15: Myths and Legends Surrounding Isis 79

Chapter 16: Comparative Mythology: Isis and Other Goddesses 84

Chapter 17: The Legacy of Isis 89

Chapter 18: Isis and Alchemy 94

Chapter 19: Isis in Literature and Popular Culture 99

Chapter 20: Embodying the Wisdom of Isis 104

Chapter 1: The Enigma of Isis

In the pantheon of ancient Egyptian deities, few figures are as enigmatic and profoundly influential as Isis. Revered as a goddess of love, healing, and magic, her legacy has traversed borders and epochs, embedding itself into the fabric of both ancient and modern cultures. This chapter delves into the mysterious allure of Isis, exploring her origins, her multifaceted roles in Egyptian mythology, and her enduring significance in the tapestry of human spirituality.

The Genesis of a Goddess

Isis's story begins in the swirling chaos of the ancient Egyptian creation myths. According to these tales, she was born of the earth god Geb and the sky goddess Nut, alongside her siblings Osiris, Set, and Nephthys. From the very outset, Isis was depicted as a goddess of remarkable attributes — a nurturer, a protector, and a wise and cunning figure whose powers transcended the boundaries of heaven and earth.

Her portrayal in Egyptian art and inscriptions often depicted her with a throne-shaped headdress, symbolizing her status as a queen of the gods. Her wings, gracefully unfurled, were a testament to her role as a protector and guardian. Isis was also frequently shown nursing her son Horus, highlighting her aspect as a divine mother, nurturing and protective.

The Tapestry of Myths

Central to Isis's story is her relationship with her brother and consort, Osiris. This tale, rich in drama and emotion, forms the backbone of many Egyptian myths. Osiris, the benevolent ruler of Egypt, was brutally murdered and dismembered by his envious brother Set. Isis, in her unyielding love and determination, scoured the earth for Osiris's scattered remains. Upon finding them, she used her magical powers to resurrect Osiris, thereby also conceiving their son, Horus.

This myth epitomizes the essence of Isis — her steadfast loyalty, her mastery over magical arts, and her role as the bringer of life and restoration. It also illustrates her connection with death and the afterlife, as she navigates the realms of the living and the dead, embodying the cycle of life, death, and rebirth.

The Goddess of a Thousand Names

Isis's influence extended far beyond the boundaries of Egyptian mythology. She was a goddess of many names and forms, revered in various capacities by different cultures. To the Greeks, she was akin to Demeter, the goddess of harvest. The Romans venerated her as a universal mother figure and a patroness of nature and magic. Throughout the Mediterranean basin, temples were erected in her honor, and her cult spread as far as the British Isles.

In all these manifestations, Isis remained a symbol of the divine feminine — a beacon of motherhood, fertility, and the mystical arts. Her ability to traverse and unite different cultures and belief systems made her one of the most universally worshipped deities of the ancient world.

Isis in Egyptian Society

In ancient Egypt, the worship of Isis permeated every aspect of life. She was the protector of the kingdom, guiding the pharaohs and ensuring the fertility of the land. Her temples were centers of healing and learning, where priests and priestesses performed rites and rituals to invoke her blessings.

The cult of Isis also played a significant role in the lives of ordinary Egyptians. She was a guardian of women and children, a patroness of love and happiness, and a guide for the souls in the afterlife. Her festivals were celebrated with joy and fervor, marked by processions, music, and feasting.

The Enduring Legacy

The allure of Isis did not fade with the decline of the ancient Egyptian civilization. In the tapestry of human history and spirituality, she has maintained a persistent presence. Modern paganism and New Age movements have rediscovered her, finding resonance in her aspects of feminine strength, healing, and magic. She remains a figure of inspiration and empowerment, a testament to the enduring power of ancient mythology in contemporary spiritual practices.

Meditation: Connecting with Ancient Energies

As we delve into the enigma of Isis, let us connect with the ancient energies she embodies. Find a quiet space where you can sit comfortably. Close your eyes and take a deep breath. As you exhale, release any tension or distractions, grounding yourself in the present moment.

Visualize yourself on the banks of the Nile, under the vast, starlit sky. The air is filled with the gentle scent of lotus flowers, and the river flows quietly beside you. Feel the ancient land's energy pulsating beneath you, timeless and powerful.

In your mind's eye, see the figure of Isis emerging from the shimmering waters. She is resplendent, her wings unfurled, her gaze kind and wise. Feel her presence enveloping you in warmth and safety.

Now, silently ask Isis to impart her wisdom and strength to you. Whether you seek healing, love, or guidance, let her ancient energy resonate within you. Feel a sense of peace and empowerment flowing through you, as if the millennia-old connection with the divine is rekindled in your spirit.

When you are ready, slowly bring your awareness back to your surroundings. Open your eyes, carrying with you the sense of peace and connection. Remember, the legacy of Isis, though rooted in the past, is a living, breathing presence, ever ready to guide and inspire.

The story of Isis is not just a chapter in the annals of ancient mythology; it is a living narrative that continues to unfold in the hearts and minds of those who seek her wisdom. As we journey through her tales and teachings, we uncover not just the secrets of a bygone era, but also timeless truths about the human spirit and the eternal quest for understanding and connection.

Chapter 2: Isis and Osiris: A Tale of Love

In the pantheon of ancient Egyptian mythology, the love story of Isis and Osiris stands as a poignant testament to the power of love, loyalty, and resurrection. This tale, woven with the threads of passion, betrayal, and ultimate triumph, resonates through the ages, offering profound insights into the human condition and the mysteries of life and death.

The Union of Isis and Osiris

The story of Isis and Osiris begins in the fertile lands of Egypt, where they ruled as king and queen. Osiris, known for his wisdom and just rule, was deeply loved by his subjects. Isis, equally revered, was celebrated for her deep wisdom, magical prowess, and nurturing heart. Together, they brought prosperity and harmony to the land of Egypt.

Their love was not merely that of a king and queen but of deities deeply entwined in purpose and passion. Isis and Osiris were not only spouses but also soulmates, their bond transcending the physical realm. In Egyptian mythology, their union was seen as the perfect harmony of masculine and feminine energies, creating balance and stability.

The Betrayal and Death of Osiris

However, this idyllic union was not to last. Osiris's brother, Set, driven by jealousy and ambition, plotted against him. In a cunning scheme, Set tricked Osiris into lying in a beautifully crafted coffin, which he then sealed and threw into the Nile.

Isis, upon learning of her husband's demise, was consumed by grief. Her lament was so profound that it echoed through the land, resonating with every creature. Refusing to accept his death, she embarked on a relentless quest to find his body.

Her journey led her through the length and breadth of Egypt and even into the realms of the unknown.

The Search and Resurrection

Isis's search eventually led her to Byblos, where she discovered Osiris's coffin entangled in the roots of a great tree. After retrieving his body, she returned to Egypt, hiding it in the marshes of the Nile Delta. Here, using her magical powers, she resurrected Osiris, reviving him long enough to conceive their son, Horus.

This act of resurrection was more than a display of her magical abilities; it was a profound act of love, transcending the boundaries between life and death. Osiris's resurrection was not to last, however, as Set discovered and dismembered his body, scattering the pieces across Egypt.

Undeterred, Isis, accompanied by her sister Nephthys, embarked on another journey to retrieve the pieces of Osiris's body. With great care, they reassembled his body and, through her magic and the assistance of other gods, brought Osiris back to life once more. This time, Osiris became the lord of the underworld, the judge of the dead, continuing his reign in a different realm.

The Symbolism of the Tale

The story of Isis and Osiris is rich in symbolic meaning. It represents the cycle of life, death, and rebirth, a theme central to the Egyptian understanding of the world. Osiris's death and resurrection symbolized the annual flooding of the Nile, bringing fertility and life to the land.

Furthermore, their story underscores the concept of eternal love and loyalty. Isis's unwavering devotion to Osiris, her refusal to let even death part them, speaks to the strength of love as an enduring, transformative force.

The Legacy of Their Love

The love between Isis and Osiris was celebrated throughout Egypt and beyond. Temples and shrines dedicated to their tale were places of worship and pilgrimage, where devotees sought blessings in love and protection in life's transitions.

Their story also influenced the rites and rituals surrounding death and the afterlife in ancient Egypt. The promise of resurrection and eternal life, as exemplified in Osiris's revival, offered comfort and hope to the people, assuring them that death was not an end, but a transition to a different form of existence.

Meditation: Embracing Unconditional Love

As we reflect on the love story of Isis and Osiris, let us engage in a heart-opening meditation focusing on unconditional love. Find a quiet and comfortable space. Sit or lie down, closing your eyes gently. Take a few deep breaths, letting go of any tension in your body.

Visualize your heart as a blooming lotus, each petal unfolding with the warmth of love. Imagine a soft, green light emanating from your heart, expanding with each breath. This light represents the unconditional love of Isis, nurturing and all-encompassing.

Now, think of a moment of pure love in your life. It could be a tender memory with a loved one, a moment of self-acceptance, or a time you felt a deep connection with the world around you. Let this memory fill your heart, intensifying the green light.

As you bask in this light, feel it dissolving any barriers or pain in your heart. Allow yourself to feel love in its purest form – without expectations, without conditions. Let this love flow through you, healing and rejuvenating every part of your being.

In this space of love, silently repeat to yourself: "I am open to love in all its forms. I give love freely, and I receive love gratefully." Feel these words resonating with the energy of Isis, reinforcing the bonds of love in your life.

When you feel ready, gently bring your awareness back to the present. Open your eyes, carrying with you the warmth and light of unconditional love.

The tale of Isis and Osiris, with its profound implications of love, loss, and rebirth, continues to be a source of inspiration and awe. It reminds us of the enduring power of love and the resilience of the human spirit in the face of life's trials. As we navigate our own journeys, their story serves as a beacon, guiding us towards the transformative power of love and the eternal cycle of renewal and regeneration.

Chapter 3: The Magical Powers of Isis

In the annals of ancient Egyptian mythology, Isis stands as a paramount figure of magic and mystical powers. Her abilities, revered and feared, were believed to extend beyond the realms of mortals, touching the domains of the gods and the universe itself. This chapter explores the profound magical aspects attributed to Isis, delving into the depths of her powers and their significance in both ancient and contemporary contexts.

The Essence of Isis's Magic

Isis's magical prowess was renowned throughout Egypt and beyond. Her knowledge of magical spells and rituals was said to be so vast that even Ra, the chief of the gods, sought her counsel. Her magic was not just a tool for personal gain but was often wielded for the benefit of others, for healing, protection, and guidance.

One of the most famous legends illustrating her magical strength is how she tricked Ra into revealing his secret name. By knowing this name, Isis gained power over Ra himself, which she used not for domination but to help and heal. This story underscores her role as a wise and cunning magician, whose power lay as much in her knowledge and wit as in her supernatural abilities.

The Healer and Protector

Isis's magic was deeply intertwined with her roles as a healer and a protector. She was often invoked in spells and rituals aimed at curing diseases and warding off evil. Her protection was sought after not only by the living but also by the souls journeying into the afterlife. The "Isis knot" amulet, resembling an ankh, was commonly used in funerary rites, symbolizing her protective powers.

In her role as a healer, Isis was believed to possess a deep understanding of medicinal herbs and treatments. Her powers of healing were not limited to physical ailments but extended to the spiritual and emotional realms, offering solace and restoration to those in distress.

Isis and Nature's Magic

Isis's connection with nature and its cycles was another crucial aspect of her magical identity. She was often associated with the moon, and her powers were believed to be at their peak during specific lunar phases. Her magic was inextricably linked with the fertility of the land, the ebb and flow of the Nile, and the mysteries of birth and rebirth.

This connection with nature's forces made her a goddess of agriculture and fertility. The rituals and ceremonies dedicated to Isis often involved offerings of the earth's bounty, seeking her blessing for abundant harvests and the prosperity of the land.

The Spellcaster and the Sorceress

Isis's reputation as a formidable spellcaster and sorceress was well-established in ancient Egyptian texts. The spells attributed to her were diverse, ranging from simple charms to complex rituals involving multiple deities and intricate symbols.

Her magic was a blend of words, gestures, and the use of sacred objects, each element integral to the success of the spell.

The power of Isis's spells lay not just in their efficacy but in the wisdom with which they were used. She was a goddess who understood the responsibility that came with such power, and her magical practices were marked by a deep respect for the balance and harmony of the universe.

The Influence of Isis's Magic

The magical legacy of Isis transcended the boundaries of ancient Egypt, influencing other cultures and traditions. In the Greco-Roman world, the cult of Isis incorporated elements of her magic into their rituals and practices. In the esoteric traditions of the later ages, Isis became a symbol of the divine feminine and the mysteries of the occult.

Her influence is seen in the rituals of modern witchcraft and pagan practices, where her aspects of magic, healing, and protection continue to be revered. The archetype of Isis serves as a source of inspiration and empowerment for those seeking to tap into their own magical potential.

Meditation: Harnessing Personal Power

As we explore the magical realms of Isis, let us engage in a visualization meditation for personal empowerment. Find a quiet space where you can relax without interruption. Sit comfortably and close your eyes. Take a few deep breaths, grounding yourself in the present moment.

Visualize yourself in an ancient temple dedicated to Isis. The walls are adorned with hieroglyphs, and the air is fragrant with incense. In the center of the temple, see a radiant figure of Isis, majestic and powerful.

Approach her and feel her welcoming presence enveloping you. She hands you an ankh, the symbol of life and magical power. As you take it, feel a surge of energy coursing through you, awakening your inner strength and potential.

Now, envision a personal goal or a challenge you wish to overcome. Hold this vision in your mind and see yourself harnessing the magical energy of Isis to achieve it. Feel a sense of confidence and empowerment growing within you, fueled by the wisdom and strength of the goddess.

Take a few moments to bask in this empowered state, feeling aligned with your purpose and abilities. When you are ready, gently bring your awareness back to the present. Open your eyes, carrying with you the sense of power and potential you have tapped into.

The magical powers of Isis, encompassing healing, protection, and the mysteries of the universe, offer a profound reflection on the potential within each of us. Her legacy reminds us that magic is not just an external force but an intrinsic part of our being, waiting to be awakened and harnessed. As we journey through our own lives, the magic of Isis serves as a guiding light, illuminating the path to empowerment and self-realization.

Chapter 4: Isis as a Healing Goddess

In the annals of ancient Egyptian mythology, Isis's role as a healer and a provider of medical knowledge stands out prominently. Her influence in the realm of healing and medicine is not just a testament to her power and wisdom, but also to the ancient Egyptians' understanding of health and well-being. This chapter delves into the multifaceted role of Isis in the domain of healing, exploring how her legacy continues to influence our perspectives on health and healing.

Isis: The Divine Healer

The character of Isis in Egyptian mythology is deeply intertwined with themes of healing and restoration. She was revered not just as a goddess who could cure physical ailments, but also as one who could heal emotional and spiritual wounds. The legend of Isis reviving her husband Osiris after his murder by Set is perhaps the most potent example of her healing powers, showcasing her ability to transcend even the boundaries of death.

Isis's healing methods were as diverse as her powers. They included the use of spells and incantations, herbal remedies, and magical objects. The ancient Egyptians believed that her knowledge of healing came directly from Thoth, the god of wisdom and writing, which included the knowledge of medicinal plants and healing techniques.

The Cult of Isis and Medicine

The worship of Isis was not confined to temples and rituals; it had a profound influence on the practice of medicine in ancient Egypt. Temples dedicated to Isis often served as centers of healing, where priests and priestesses trained in the medical arts offered treatments to the sick and injured. These healers were seen as intermediaries of Isis, channeling her healing powers.

The medical texts of ancient Egypt, such as the Ebers Papyrus, reflect the influence of Isis. These texts include a variety of medical knowledge, ranging from surgical practices to treatments for various ailments, embodying the holistic approach to health that Isis represented.

Isis's Influence Beyond Egypt

The healing powers of Isis were not limited to the boundaries of ancient Egypt. As her cult spread across the Mediterranean and into the Greco-Roman world, so did her reputation as a healer. In these cultures, she was often syncretized with local healing deities, such as the Greek goddess Demeter and the Roman goddess Ceres.

This blending of beliefs created a rich tapestry of healing practices and traditions, with Isis at the center. Her influence can be seen in the development of early medical practices in these regions, highlighting the cross-cultural impact of her healing legacy.

Healing in the Modern Context

The archetype of Isis as a healer has endured through the centuries, finding resonance in modern holistic and alternative healing practices. Her image as a nurturing, wise, and powerful healer continues to inspire those seeking a deeper understanding of health and wellness.

In contemporary spiritual practices, Isis is often invoked in rituals and meditations focused on healing and well-being. Her legacy serves as a reminder of the interconnectedness of physical, emotional, and spiritual health, encouraging a holistic approach to healing.

Meditation: Embracing Isis's Healing Energy

In honor of Isis's role as a healing goddess, let us engage in a meditation focused on physical and emotional well-being. Find a quiet, comfortable space where you can sit or lie down. Close your eyes and take deep, slow breaths, allowing your body to relax with each exhale.

Visualize yourself in a tranquil garden, a sacred space dedicated to Isis. The air is filled with the fragrance of healing herbs, and a gentle breeze caresses your skin. In the center of the garden stands a beautiful statue of Isis, radiant and serene.

Approach the statue and feel a sense of peace enveloping you. As you stand in her presence, visualize a soft, nurturing light emanating from the statue, enveloping you in its warm embrace. This light is the healing energy of Isis, soothing and restorative.

Now, focus on any area of your body or aspect of your life that needs healing. It could be a physical ailment, emotional pain, or a stressful situation. Visualize the healing light of Isis flowing into this area or situation, bringing comfort, healing, and balance.

Feel the light dissolving any pain, tension, or negativity, replacing it with a sense of well-being and harmony. Allow yourself to be immersed in this healing energy, trusting in the nurturing power of Isis to restore and rejuvenate.

When you feel ready, gently bring your awareness back to the present. Open your eyes, carrying with you the sense of healing and peace you have experienced.

The role of Isis as a healing goddess in ancient Egyptian mythology offers profound insights into the timeless quest for health and well-being. Her legacy reminds us of the power of holistic healing, embracing the physical, emotional, and spiritual dimensions of our lives. As we navigate our own paths to health and healing, the wisdom and energy of Isis serve as a guiding light, illuminating the way to balance and restoration.

Chapter 5: Isis in the Everyday Life of Ancient Egypt

In the ancient world, the presence of gods and goddesses was not confined to temples and grandiose myths; they were an integral part of daily life, guiding and influencing every aspect of existence. Among these deities, Isis held a special place in the hearts and lives of the ancient Egyptians. This chapter explores how Isis was revered and worshipped in the everyday life of the ancient Egyptians, revealing her enduring influence on their culture, rituals, and personal beliefs.

Isis: A Goddess for All

Isis was a deity who transcended social and economic boundaries. Her worship was not limited to the pharaohs and the priesthood but was widespread among the common people as well. She was accessible to everyone, from the mightiest king to the humblest peasant, making her one of the most universally venerated deities in ancient Egypt.

Her appeal lay in her multifaceted nature; she was a mother, a wife, a healer, and a protector. This made her relatable and revered in various aspects of daily life. Women, in particular, looked up to her as a model of motherly and wifely virtues, praying to her for fertility, protection during childbirth, and assistance in domestic affairs.

The Protector of the Household

In many Egyptian homes, small altars or shrines were dedicated to Isis. These were places where families would offer prayers and small offerings, seeking her blessings and protection. Amulets bearing her image or symbols were common, worn for protection against harm and to bring good fortune.

The role of Isis as a protector extended beyond the living. She was also seen as a guardian of the dead, ensuring safe passage into the afterlife. This made her an important figure in funerary practices, with prayers and rituals dedicated to her for the deceased.

Festivals and Celebrations

Festivals in honor of Isis were among the most significant religious events in ancient Egypt. These festivals were not just religious ceremonies but also social and cultural gatherings, bringing communities together in celebration and worship.

One of the most important festivals was the 'Feast of the Beautiful Meeting,' which celebrated the annual reunion of Isis and Osiris. This festival involved processions carrying the statues of Isis and Osiris, reflecting the mythological journey of Isis in search of her husband. It was a time of joy and celebration, symbolizing the triumph of love and the renewal of life.

The Agricultural Connection

Isis was closely associated with agriculture and the Nile's annual flooding, which was crucial for Egypt's fertility. Farmers prayed to her for successful harvests, and rituals were performed in her honor to ensure the Nile's timely inundation. This connection with the life-giving aspects of the Nile further cemented her status as a nurturing and life-sustaining deity.

Personal Devotion

Personal devotion to Isis often involved prayers and incantations. These prayers were intimate communications between the individual and the goddess, expressing personal hopes, fears, and gratitude. The ancient Egyptians believed that Isis, with her deep wisdom and understanding, would listen to and aid them in their troubles and aspirations.

The Legacy in Art and Literature

The reverence for Isis was reflected in Egyptian art and literature. She was a popular subject in paintings, sculptures, and literary works, often depicted as a beautiful woman wearing a throne-shaped headdress or with wings spread in protection. These artistic representations were not just decorative but served as a means of honoring and invoking her presence.

Meditation: Embracing the Present with Isis

Inspired by ancient Egyptian practices, let us engage in a mindfulness meditation to connect with the essence of Isis in our daily lives. Find a quiet place where you can sit comfortably without distractions. Close your eyes and take a few deep breaths, allowing your body to relax.

Imagine yourself on the banks of the Nile, the lifeblood of ancient Egypt. Feel the gentle breeze and hear the rustle of papyrus reeds. Visualize the sun setting over the river, casting a golden glow on the water.

In this tranquil setting, picture the presence of Isis. See her as a symbol of strength, wisdom, and nurturing love. Feel her calming energy surrounding you, bringing peace and balance to your mind and spirit.

Now, bring your focus to the present moment. Be aware of your breath, the sensations in your body, the sounds around you. Let any thoughts or worries gently drift away like boats on the Nile. In this space of mindfulness, find a deep connection with the here and now, feeling grounded and centered.

As you sit in this peaceful state, reflect on the aspects of your life where you can invoke the qualities of Isis. It might be seeking balance in your daily tasks, strength in facing challenges, or offering nurturing love to those around you.

When you are ready, gently bring your awareness back to your surroundings. Open your eyes, carrying with you the serenity and strength you have found in this meditation.

The presence of Isis in the everyday life of ancient Egyptians was a testament to their deep connection with the divine in their daily existence. She was not a distant figure but a constant companion, guiding and influencing every aspect of their lives. Her legacy reminds us of the power of integrating spiritual beliefs and practices into our daily routines, enriching our lives with meaning and purpose.

Chapter 6: Symbols of Isis

In the rich tapestry of Egyptian mythology, symbols carry profound meanings, encapsulating the essence of the gods and their powers. Among these, the symbols associated with Isis are particularly evocative, offering deep insights into her nature and influence. This chapter explores the most significant symbols of Isis, delving into their origins, meanings, and the ways in which they were revered in ancient times.

The Throne: Symbol of Power and Authority

One of the most recognizable symbols of Isis is the throne. Often depicted in hieroglyphs and artworks as a throne-shaped headdress worn by the goddess, it represents her role as the mother of Horus, the pharaohs' divine mother. This symbolizes not just physical motherhood but also the idea of Isis as the source of legitimate power and authority. The throne as a symbol underscores her importance in the pharaonic lineage, signifying her protective and nurturing role over the rulers of Egypt.

The Ankh: Symbol of Life

The ankh, a key symbol of life in ancient Egyptian culture, is closely associated with Isis. Often seen in depictions of the goddess holding an ankh to the pharaoh's nose, symbolizing the breath of life, it represents her role as a giver of life and a healer. The ankh in the hands of Isis becomes a powerful emblem of her ability to grant life and to resurrect, as she did with Osiris.

The Knot of Isis: Symbol of Protection

The tyet, also known as the Knot of Isis, resembles an ankh with its arms at its side. This symbol, often made into amulets, was believed to offer protection, particularly in the afterlife. It was closely linked with the menstrual cloth of Isis, symbolizing the magical properties of the goddess's feminine aspects. The Knot of Isis, therefore, represents the divine protection offered by Isis, serving as a guardian against evil and misfortune.

The Wings of Isis: Symbol of Protection and Embrace

Isis is frequently depicted with wings, which she used to fan breath and life back into Osiris. These wings symbolize her role as a protective goddess, who spreads her wings to offer shelter and comfort. In many tomb paintings and sarcophagi, Isis's wings are shown outspread as a protective embrace over the deceased, ensuring their safe journey to the afterlife.

The Sycamore Tree: Symbol of Provision and Protection

The sycamore tree was sacred to Isis and was often depicted in funerary art. According to myth, Isis, in the guise of a sycamore tree, provided food and water to the spirits of the dead. This symbolizes her nurturing aspect and her role as a provider of sustenance and protection.

The Moon and the Stars: Symbols of Magic and Motherhood

Isis was often associated with the moon and the stars, symbols that reflect her attributes as a goddess of magic and motherhood. The waxing and waning of the moon were seen as representations of the cycles of life and death, a theme central to the myth of Isis and Osiris. The stars were thought to be the souls of the dead, over whom Isis, as a celestial mother, watched and provided guidance.

Meditation: Journey Through the Symbols of Isis

Let us embark on a guided imagery meditation to connect with the symbols of Isis. Find a quiet place where you can relax and close your eyes. Breathe deeply and steadily, allowing yourself to sink into a state of calm.

Visualize yourself standing at the edge of the Nile at dusk. The water is calm, reflecting the soft light of the setting sun. In front of you, a path lined with sycamore trees leads to an ancient temple dedicated to Isis.

As you walk this path, notice a beautiful ankh carved into the bark of each tree, glowing with a soft light. Feel the energy of life emanating from these symbols, filling you with vitality and strength.

Upon reaching the temple, you see a massive pair of wings, the wings of Isis, carved into the temple doors. As the doors open, feel the protective embrace of Isis surrounding you, offering shelter and comfort.

Inside the temple, you find a throne at the center. Sit upon it and feel the power and wisdom of Isis filling you. You are in the presence of the divine, imbued with authority and compassion.

Now, look up at the temple ceiling, painted as a night sky with stars and a luminous moon. As you gaze at it, feel the magic and maternal love of Isis washing over you, nurturing and guiding you.

Take a few moments to bask in the presence of these symbols, letting their energies infuse your being. When you are ready, gently bring yourself back to the present, carrying with you the strength and protection of Isis.

The symbols of Isis are more than mere representations; they are conduits of her power and essence. Through understanding and connecting with these symbols, we tap into the ancient wisdom and protection of one of the most revered deities in Egyptian mythology, bringing her timeless influence into our lives.

Chapter 7: Isis and the Afterlife

The ancient Egyptians held a profound belief in the afterlife, a realm where the soul would journey after death. This belief system was intricately woven with their deities, rituals, and daily practices, with Isis playing a pivotal role in the journey of the soul into the afterlife. Her influence in funeral practices and beliefs about the afterlife is an essential aspect of understanding her role in ancient Egyptian religion. This chapter explores Isis's role in the afterlife, her influence on funeral practices, and the comfort she provided to the souls of the departed.

Isis: The Divine Guide to the Afterlife

In the tapestry of Egyptian mythology, Isis's role as a guide and protector in the afterlife is central. Her own experience with death and resurrection, through the story of Osiris, made her a symbol of hope and renewal for the dead. As Osiris became the ruler of the underworld, Isis, his consort, was often invoked to aid and protect the souls as they made their journey into the afterlife.

Isis in Funeral Practices

Isis's influence permeated Egyptian funeral practices. Her image and symbols were a common sight in tombs and on sarcophagi, where they were believed to offer protection and guidance to the deceased. Prayers and spells from the "Book of the Dead" often called upon Isis to use her powers to ensure safe passage for the soul and to help it overcome the trials of the afterlife.

One of the most significant roles of Isis in funeral practices was her association with the "Opening of the Mouth" ceremony. This ritual, performed on the mummy by priests, was believed to restore the senses of the deceased so they could interact with the world of the living and the gods. Isis, known for her restorative powers, was a central figure in this ceremony, ensuring the deceased's ability to breathe, eat, and speak in the afterlife.

The Comforter of the Mourning

Isis was not only a guide for the dead but also a comforter for the living who mourned. Her own grief for Osiris resonated with the emotions of those who lost loved ones. She was often depicted in mourning, an image that offered solace to the bereaved, reminding them that they were not alone in their sorrow. The empathy she embodied provided a sense of connection and understanding, making her an approachable deity in times of grief.

The Protector of Children and the Vulnerable

Isis's protective nature extended to children and the vulnerable, both in life and death. She was seen as a guardian of the innocent, ensuring their safety and well-being in the afterlife. Her maternal instincts made her a compassionate figure who watched over the souls of the young and the weak, offering them her care and protection.

Isis and the Immortality of the Soul

The beliefs surrounding Isis and the afterlife also reflected the Egyptian view of the soul's immortality. Through her magical powers and deep understanding of the mysteries of life and death, Isis was seen as a key figure in the soul's eternal journey. Her role in resurrecting Osiris was a direct metaphor for the rebirth of the soul, offering a promise of continual existence beyond physical death.

Meditation: Contemplating Life, Death, and Rebirth

In the spirit of Isis's role in the afterlife, let us engage in a reflective meditation on life, death, and rebirth. Find a quiet place where you can sit or lie down comfortably. Close your eyes and take a few deep breaths, allowing your body to relax.

Visualize a vast, starlit sky above you, reminiscent of the Egyptian belief in the celestial journey of the soul. Under this sky, see yourself standing at the edge of the Nile, the river symbolizing the flow of life and the passage of time.

Contemplate the river's journey from its source to the sea, mirroring the journey of life. Reflect on your own life path, the experiences that have shaped you, the joys and sorrows, the beginnings and endings.

Now, turn your thoughts to the concept of death, not as an end, but as a transition. Imagine Isis, with her comforting presence, guiding you through this transition. Feel her empathy and understanding, reassuring you of the continuity of the soul.

As you contemplate rebirth, envision a lotus flower blooming on the Nile, a symbol of regeneration and new beginnings. Reflect on the cycles of your own life, the opportunities for growth and renewal, and the perpetual journey of the soul. Take a few moments to sit with these reflections, feeling a sense of peace and understanding about the cycles of life, death, and rebirth. When you are ready, gently bring your awareness back to the present, carrying with you the insights and tranquility you have gained.

Isis's role in the afterlife in ancient Egyptian culture provides a profound perspective on the continuity of life and the eternal journey of the soul. Her presence in funeral practices and her role as a guide and protector in the afterlife offer comfort and assurance in the face of life's greatest mystery. Her legacy in this realm continues to inspire and provide a deeper understanding of the cycles of existence.

Chapter 8: The Priesthood of Isis

The worship of Isis, one of the most prominent deities in ancient Egyptian mythology, was upheld and propagated by a dedicated priesthood. This chapter explores the roles, rituals, and significance of the priests and priestesses of Isis, delving into their practices, the intricacies of their ceremonies, and their influence on the spiritual and daily life of ancient Egyptians.

The Role of the Priesthood

In ancient Egypt, the priesthood played a pivotal role in maintaining the relationship between the gods and the people. The priests and priestesses of Isis were no exception; they served as intermediaries between the goddess and her devotees. Their duties extended beyond the temple walls, encompassing education, healing, and the preservation of sacred knowledge.

Selection and Training

The process of becoming a priest or priestess of Isis was rigorous and steeped in tradition. Candidates were often chosen based on specific criteria, including lineage, purity, and devotion to the goddess. Training for the priesthood involved learning complex rituals, sacred texts, and healing practices. This education ensured that the priests and priestesses were not only religious leaders but also custodians of cultural and spiritual heritage.

Daily Rituals and Ceremonies

The daily rituals performed by the priesthood were central to the worship of Isis. These rituals included the purification of the temple, offerings of food and incense, and recitations of hymns and prayers. The most sacred ritual was the "divine liturgy," performed daily, wherein the statue of Isis was clothed, anointed, and presented with offerings. This ritual symbolized the eternal care and attention the goddess received from her followers.

Festivals and Public Ceremonies

In addition to daily rituals, the priesthood of Isis organized and led grand festivals and ceremonies. These events were often public, allowing the wider community to participate in the worship and celebration of the goddess. Festivals such as the "Feast of the Beautiful Meeting," which celebrated the reunion of Isis and Osiris, were occasions of great joy and festivity, involving processions, music, and communal feasting.

The Healing Role

The priests and priestesses of Isis were renowned for their healing abilities. Drawing on the goddess's association with health and healing, they often acted as physicians, using herbs, spells, and prayers to cure ailments. The temples of Isis served as centers of healing, where people sought relief from physical and spiritual maladies.

The Mysteries of Isis

The priesthood was also responsible for maintaining and conducting the "Mysteries of Isis," a set of complex rituals and teachings that offered deeper spiritual insights into the nature of the goddess and the universe. These mysteries were considered highly sacred and were often shrouded in secrecy, revealed only to initiates who had proven their devotion and understanding.

The Spread of the Cult of Isis

The influence of the priesthood of Isis extended far beyond Egypt. As her cult spread across the Mediterranean and into Europe, the priests and priestesses played a crucial role in adapting and integrating Isis worship into local cultures. This expansion led to the formation of a diverse and widespread community of devotees, united by their reverence for the goddess.

Meditation: Connecting with the Divine Feminine

In honor of the ancient priesthood of Isis, let us engage in a devotional meditation to connect with the divine feminine. Find a quiet place where you can sit comfortably. Close your eyes and take deep, steady breaths, centering yourself.

Visualize yourself in an ancient temple of Isis, surrounded by flickering candles and the scent of incense. In the center of the temple, see a statue of Isis, radiant and majestic.

Approach the statue and offer a silent prayer or intention, feeling a connection with the goddess. As you stand before her, visualize a gentle, nurturing light emanating from the statue, enveloping you in warmth and love.

Feel this light penetrating your being, awakening the qualities of the divine feminine within you – compassion, wisdom, strength, and intuition. Reflect on these qualities and how you can embody them in your daily life.

Take a few moments to bask in the presence of Isis, feeling a deep sense of connection with the divine feminine. When you are ready, gently bring your awareness back to the present, carrying with you the insights and tranquility you have gained.

The priesthood of Isis played a crucial role in maintaining and spreading the worship of one of ancient Egypt's most revered deities. Their rituals, knowledge, and devotion not only honored the goddess but also enriched the spiritual and cultural fabric of their society. The legacy of these priests and priestesses continues to inspire those who seek a deeper understanding of the divine feminine and the ancient mysteries of the world.

Chapter 9: The Spread of Isis's Cult

The worship of Isis, originating in the fertile lands of ancient Egypt, transcended its geographical and cultural boundaries, evolving into a widespread and enduring religious movement. This chapter delves into the spread of the cult of Isis beyond Egypt, tracing its journey through different civilizations, the adaptations it underwent, and its lasting impact on various cultures.

The Roots in Egypt

The cult of Isis began in ancient Egypt, where she was revered as a goddess of magic, motherhood, and fertility. Her worship was integral to Egyptian religion and culture, with her mythology deeply embedded in the Egyptian conception of the cosmos, life, and the afterlife.

The Hellenistic World

The spread of Isis's worship began significantly during the Hellenistic period, particularly after the conquests of Alexander the Great. This era saw a fusion of Greek and Egyptian cultures, with the city of Alexandria becoming a melting pot of beliefs and ideas. Isis, known to the Greeks as Isis of Ten Thousand Names, was syncretized with Greek goddesses like Demeter and Aphrodite, embodying aspects of motherhood, agriculture, and love.

The Roman Empire

The cult of Isis found fertile ground in the Roman Empire, where it flourished from around the first century BCE onwards. Her appeal in the Roman world lay in her universal qualities – as a protector, a mother, and a bringer of life. Temples dedicated to Isis sprang up throughout the empire, from Britain to the far reaches of North Africa. The festival of Isia, marking the death and resurrection of Osiris, became a popular celebration, symbolizing the eternal cycle of life and death.

Adaptation and Integration

As the cult of Isis spread, it adapted to local cultures and religious practices. In Greece and Rome, she was often depicted in a manner similar to local goddesses, and her myths were interpreted through the lens of local beliefs. This syncretism made her worship appealing to a wide range of people, from different social and cultural backgrounds.

The Mystery Cults

One of the key aspects of Isis's worship outside Egypt was its transformation into a mystery cult. These mystery cults, particularly prominent in Greece and Rome, offered personal salvation and the promise of life after death. Initiates underwent secret rituals and ceremonies, which were believed to bring them closer to the divine and grant them a deeper understanding of the mysteries of life.

The Decline and Legacy

The spread of Christianity in the Roman Empire eventually led to the decline of the cult of Isis.

However, her influence did not disappear. The figure of Isis, especially her aspects as a merciful mother and protector, left a lasting mark on Christian iconography and theology. The Black Madonna, venerated in various Christian traditions, is often seen as a continuation of the worship of Isis.

Meditation: Embracing Interconnectedness

In light of the spread of the cult of Isis, let us engage in a meditation focused on interconnectedness and cultural exchange. Find a quiet and comfortable place to sit or lie down. Close your eyes and take a few deep breaths, centering yourself in the present moment.

Imagine yourself standing at the crossroads of ancient civilizations – in the bustling streets of Alexandria, the grandeur of Rome, or the sacred temples of Greece. As you stand here, visualize people from all walks of life and different cultures passing by, each bringing their beliefs, traditions, and stories.

Reflect on the figure of Isis as she appears in these various cultures. See her as a symbol of unity and diversity, embodying different aspects to different people, yet maintaining her core essence. Feel a sense of connection with the diverse followers of Isis, understanding that despite our differences, we share common hopes, fears, and aspirations.

Contemplate the idea of cultural exchange – how beliefs, ideas, and traditions travel and evolve, enriching societies and fostering understanding. Think about the role you play in this ongoing exchange of ideas and beliefs in your own life.

Take a few moments to bask in this sense of interconnectedness, feeling a bond with the past and the present, the near and the far. When you are ready, gently bring yourself back to the present, carrying with you a sense of unity and appreciation for the diverse tapestry of human culture.

The spread of Isis's cult is a testament to the power of cultural exchange and the enduring appeal of universal themes like love, protection, and rebirth. Her journey from the banks of the Nile to the far reaches of the ancient world reflects the interconnectedness of human societies and the shared spiritual quest that transcends geographical and cultural boundaries.

Chapter 10: Isis in Modern Spirituality

In the contemporary spiritual landscape, the figure of Isis has experienced a remarkable resurgence. This revival is part of a broader reawakening of interest in ancient deities, as modern seekers look to the past for inspiration and wisdom. This chapter explores the role of Isis in modern spirituality, examining how her ancient mythology resonates with contemporary audiences and the ways in which she is invoked in modern practices.

The Relevance of Ancient Myths

In a world where traditional religious structures are often questioned, many people have turned to ancient mythologies for spiritual guidance. Isis, with her rich and multifaceted persona, offers a compelling figure for modern worship. Her roles as a nurturing mother, a wise magician, and a resilient goddess who overcomes great trials speak to the contemporary quest for empowerment, wisdom, and understanding.

Isis in Neopaganism and Wicca

Neopagan and Wiccan traditions have played a significant role in the resurgence of Isis in modern spirituality. In these paths, she is revered as a manifestation of the divine feminine, an embodiment of nature, and a symbol of fertility and magic. Her story of death and rebirth is particularly resonant in these traditions, symbolizing the cycles of nature and the human experience.

Feminism and the Divine Feminine

The rise of feminist spirituality has also contributed to the renewed interest in Isis. In her, many find a powerful symbol of female empowerment, autonomy, and resilience. Her mythology, which includes profound themes of love, loss, and rebirth, is seen as an allegory for the experiences and struggles of women throughout history. As a goddess who held her own in a pantheon dominated by male deities, Isis represents the strength and potential of the divine feminine.

Isis in Contemporary Rituals

Modern practitioners often incorporate elements of ancient Egyptian rituals into their worship of Isis, adapting them to fit contemporary spiritual needs. These rituals can include the use of symbols such as the ankh and the sistrum, the recitation of hymns and prayers from ancient texts, and the enactment of mythological stories. These practices are not mere recreations of the past but are imbued with personal and modern significance.

Isis in Art and Popular Culture

The image of Isis has permeated modern art and popular culture, further increasing her visibility and appeal. She appears in literature, movies, music, and even fashion, often as a symbol of mystery, power, and enduring grace. This cultural presence has helped introduce her to a broader audience, making her stories and symbolism accessible to those outside traditional spiritual paths.

Meditation: Invoking the Presence of Isis

In keeping with the theme of Isis in modern spirituality, let us engage in a meditation designed to invoke her presence and wisdom. Find a quiet place where you can sit comfortably without distractions. Close your eyes, take a deep breath, and relax your body.

Visualize yourself in a peaceful garden at twilight, the time when the ancient Egyptians believed the veil between worlds was thinnest. In the center of the garden, imagine an altar dedicated to Isis, adorned with symbols such as the ankh, a full moon, and blue lotuses.

As you approach the altar, feel a sense of reverence and openness. Light an imaginary candle on the altar, and as you do, call upon Isis to join you in this sacred space. Say, either aloud or in your mind, "Great Isis, goddess of magic and wisdom, I invoke your presence."

Visualize a soft light emanating from the altar, growing brighter and warmer. Feel the presence of Isis enveloping the garden, her energy radiating strength, compassion, and understanding. Allow yourself to bask in her presence, absorbing her qualities of resilience, wisdom, and nurturing love.

Ask Isis for guidance, insight, or support on a personal issue or a spiritual question. Listen with your heart for her response, which may come as a thought, a feeling, or an intuitive knowing.

When your communion feels complete, express your gratitude to Isis for her presence and wisdom. Watch as the light from the altar slowly fades, leaving you with a sense of peace and empowerment.

Gently bring your awareness back to the present moment. Open your eyes, carrying with you the insights and energies you have received.

The resurgence of Isis in modern spirituality represents a bridge between the ancient and the contemporary, offering timeless wisdom and a connection to the divine feminine. Her enduring appeal lies in her ability to adapt to different cultural and spiritual landscapes, providing guidance, strength, and inspiration to a diverse array of followers in today's world.

Chapter 11: Isis and Her Siblings

In the intricate web of ancient Egyptian mythology, the relationships between deities often reflect complex human emotions and dynamics. Among these divine relationships, the interactions between Isis and her siblings - Osiris, Set, and Nephthys - are particularly fascinating, offering rich insights into themes of loyalty, betrayal, love, and redemption. This chapter delves into the multifaceted relationships between Isis and her siblings, exploring how these interactions shaped their myths and influenced ancient Egyptian culture.

Isis and Osiris: A Bond of Love and Loyalty

The relationship between Isis and Osiris is perhaps the most celebrated and poignant among the Egyptian gods. As husband and wife, their love story transcends the physical world, embodying the ideals of devotion and eternal love. Isis's loyalty to Osiris is legendary; after his murder by Set, she tirelessly searches for his body, restores it, and brings him back to life.

Their union is not just a romantic bond but also a partnership of ruling and nurturing the land and its people. Osiris, as the god of fertility and resurrection, and Isis, as the goddess of magic and motherhood, complement each other, creating harmony and balance.

Isis and Set: Adversaries and the Balance of Power

The relationship between Isis and Set is marked by tension and opposition. Set, the god of chaos, envy, and destruction, is the antithesis of Isis's nurturing and protective nature. His murder of Osiris and subsequent conflict with Horus, the son of Isis and Osiris, places Isis in direct opposition to her brother.

However, this adversarial relationship also brings balance to the Egyptian pantheon. Set's chaotic nature contrasts with Isis's order and stability, highlighting the ancient Egyptians' belief in the necessity of balance between opposing forces in the universe.

Isis and Nephthys: Sisterhood and Support

Nephthys, often overshadowed by her more famous sister, shares a complex yet profound bond with Isis. As sisters, they are often depicted together, providing mutual support in times of crisis. Nephthys, despite being married to Set, aids Isis in the search for Osiris's body and the upbringing of Horus, showing solidarity against Set's destructive actions.

This relationship between Isis and Nephthys symbolizes the power of sisterhood and the strength found in unity. Their cooperation and shared dedication to restoring balance and order exemplify the importance of family bonds, even in the face of adversity.

The Collective Influence of the Sibling Dynamics

The dynamics between Isis and her siblings are not just individual relationships but also reflect broader themes in Egyptian mythology. These interactions encompass the duality of nature, the cycle of life and death, and the struggle between order and chaos. The myths surrounding these deities are woven into the fabric of ancient Egyptian culture, influencing religious beliefs, rituals, and the societal understanding of familial roles and relationships.

Meditation: Finding Balance in Family Dynamics

In light of the complex relationships between Isis and her siblings, let us engage in a meditation focusing on balance within our own family dynamics. Find a comfortable and quiet place to sit or lie down. Close your eyes, take deep breaths, and allow your body to relax.

Visualize a tranquil garden, a space of harmony and peace. In this garden, imagine a large, sturdy tree representing your family tree, with branches extending in all directions.

See yourself sitting under this tree, feeling grounded and connected to its roots. Reflect on your own family relationships, acknowledging the different dynamics, the love, the challenges, and the support.

As you ponder these relationships, visualize a gentle light emanating from your heart, extending towards the tree. This light symbolizes understanding, compassion, and the desire for harmony. Imagine this light reaching each branch, soothing conflicts, strengthening bonds, and nurturing growth.

Contemplate the idea that, like the relationship between Isis and her siblings, family dynamics are complex and multifaceted, yet essential for growth and balance. Recognize the value of each relationship, with its unique challenges and contributions to your life.

Take a few moments to sit with these reflections, feeling a sense of peace and balance within your family dynamics. When you are ready, gently bring your awareness back to the present, carrying with you the insights and tranquility you have gained.

The relationships between Isis and her siblings offer a window into the ancient Egyptians' views on family, power, and the natural order. These mythological narratives provide timeless insights into the complexities of familial bonds, reminding us of the enduring impact of these relationships on our lives and communities.

Chapter 12: The Festivals of Isis

In ancient Egypt, festivals were not only times of celebration but also crucial aspects of religious life, marking significant moments in the mythological and natural cycles. Among the most important and vibrant were the festivals dedicated to Isis, the goddess of magic, motherhood, and fertility. These festivals, rich in symbolism and communal participation, played a vital role in honoring the goddess and securing her blessings. This chapter explores the nature and significance of these festivals, providing a glimpse into the ancient world's spiritual and cultural life.

The Feast of the Beautiful Meeting

One of the most significant festivals in honor of Isis was the "Feast of the Beautiful Meeting." This annual celebration marked the mythological meeting of Isis with her husband Osiris. According to the myth, Isis would journey to visit the body of Osiris, symbolizing the reuniting of the living and the dead, and the renewal of life and fertility.

The festival involved elaborate processions where the statues of Isis and Osiris were carried out of their temples and brought together, symbolizing their annual reunion. The processions were accompanied by music, dancing, and the singing of hymns. The people would participate joyously, reflecting the belief that this union brought about the flooding of the Nile, which was essential for agriculture.

The Festival of Khoiak

The Festival of Khoiak, closely associated with the cult of Osiris but significant for Isis worshippers as well, was celebrated during the inundation of the Nile. It involved the creation of 'Osiris beds' - figurines of Osiris made from soil and grain seeds, which were watered until they germinated. This practice symbolized the resurrection of Osiris and the life-giving fertility he brought to the land. For Isis worshippers, this festival reinforced her role as the bringer of life and her connection to the earth's fertility.

The Night of the Tear-Drop

Another festival was the "Night of the Tear-Drop," a commemoration of the tears Isis shed for Osiris, which were believed to contribute to the flooding of the Nile. It was a time of reflection on the themes of loss, love, and the regenerative power of water. Rituals involved pouring libations and the offering of small boats adorned with lights onto the river, symbolizing the journey of Isis and her tears.

The Festival of the Lamps

The Festival of the Lamps was held at night, where worshippers would light thousands of lamps around their homes, in temples, and along the Nile. This festival was not only a visual spectacle but also a spiritual event. The lamps were symbols of the light of Isis, penetrating the darkness and guiding souls in the afterlife. It was a time to honor the dead and to celebrate the protective and illuminating power of the goddess.

Celebratory Meditation: Aligning with Nature's Cycles

In the spirit of the ancient festivals of Isis, let us engage in a celebratory meditation that aligns us with the cycles of nature. Find a quiet place where you can relax. Sit comfortably and close your eyes. Begin by taking deep, slow breaths, allowing yourself to feel centered and calm.

Visualize yourself in an ancient Egyptian landscape, standing beside the Nile at the time of its flooding. Feel the energy of life and renewal that the river brings to the land. Imagine the festivities around you, with music, dancing, and the joyous processions of Isis and Osiris.

As you immerse yourself in this celebratory atmosphere, reflect on the cycle of life and the rhythms of nature. Contemplate the ebb and flow of your own life experiences, recognizing the natural cycles of growth, change, and renewal.

Feel a sense of connection with the ancient worshippers of Isis, sharing in their reverence for the natural world and the divine. Embrace the joy and vitality that come with this connection, feeling it rejuvenate and energize your spirit.

Take a few moments to enjoy this state of celebration and unity with nature. When you are ready, gently bring your awareness back to the present, carrying with you the joy and energy of this meditative celebration.

The festivals dedicated to Isis in ancient Egypt were more than mere religious observances; they were vital expressions of a culture deeply intertwined with the rhythms of the natural world and the divine. Today, they continue to inspire us, reminding us of the power of communal celebration, the reverence for nature, and the enduring legacy of ancient spirituality.

Chapter 13: Isis in Art and Iconography

The depiction of Isis in ancient Egyptian art and iconography is rich and varied, reflecting her multifaceted nature and the significant role she played in the religious and cultural life of ancient Egypt. This chapter explores the various artistic representations of Isis, examining their symbolism, evolution, and the insights they offer into ancient Egyptian religion and mythology.

Early Depictions of Isis

In the earliest artistic representations, Isis is depicted in a manner typical of Egyptian goddesses – as a woman wearing a sheath dress and a throne-shaped headdress, symbolizing her role as the throne of Egypt and the mother of Horus, the pharaoh. These early depictions emphasize her status as a royal mother figure and a goddess of power and authority.

The Symbolism of the Throne

The throne headdress is one of the most distinctive attributes of Isis in Egyptian art. It represents her connection to the pharaohs and her role in legitimizing their rule. The throne symbolizes stability and continuity, reflecting Isis's role as a protector of the royal lineage and the sustainer of the pharaonic order.

Isis and the Sistrum

Isis is often depicted holding a sistrum, a musical instrument associated with fertility and joy. The sistrum's rattling sound was believed to drive away evil spirits and to please the gods. In the hands of Isis, it symbolizes her role in promoting life and warding off chaos.

The Wings of Isis

Another common representation of Isis in art and iconography is that of a winged goddess. These wings were sometimes outstretched in a protective gesture, especially in funerary contexts, where she was believed to protect and guide the deceased in the afterlife. The wings also symbolize her role as a divine mother, offering shelter and comfort to her worshippers.

Isis and the Knot of Isis (Tyet)

The Knot of Isis, or tyet, is an emblem closely associated with the goddess and often appears in art and amulets. Resembling an ankh with its arms at its side, the tyet represents life and welfare. It is believed to have protective powers, especially in the afterlife, and is sometimes referred to as the "blood of Isis," symbolizing the magical power of her life-giving abilities.

Isis in Ptolemaic and Roman Periods

During the Ptolemaic and Roman periods, the depiction of Isis evolved, showing Hellenistic and Roman influences. She was often portrayed in a manner similar to Greek and Roman goddesses, wearing Greek-style garments and headdresses. This syncretism reflected the blending of cultures and the universal appeal of Isis across the Mediterranean world.

Isis in Contemporary Art

In modern times, the image of Isis continues to inspire artists, who often draw on ancient representations to portray her as a symbol of femininity, magic, and spiritual power. Contemporary depictions of Isis often emphasize her aspects as a nurturing mother, a wise magician, and a protector, resonating with modern spiritual and feminist themes.

Meditation: Creative Visualization Inspired by Isis

To connect with the artistic representations of Isis, let us engage in a creative visualization meditation. Find a quiet space where you can relax without interruption. Sit comfortably and close your eyes. Begin by taking deep, slow breaths to center yourself.

Visualize yourself in an ancient Egyptian temple filled with beautiful artworks of Isis. Walk through this temple, observing the different representations of the goddess – her throne headdress, her wings, and her holding the sistrum and tyet.

As you gaze upon these artworks, reflect on what each symbol represents – authority, protection, life, and magic. Feel a connection with these ancient symbols, allowing them to speak to your inner wisdom and intuition.

Now, imagine creating your own artistic representation of Isis. Visualize a canvas before you, and see yourself painting or sculpting an image of the goddess that resonates with your personal understanding and connection to her. Let this be an expression of your creativity and spiritual insight.

Take a few moments to admire your work, feeling a sense of accomplishment and connection with the divine. When you are ready, gently bring your awareness back to the present, carrying with you the inspiration and tranquility from this meditative exercise.

The artistic depictions of Isis, spanning thousands of years, offer a window into the religious and cultural world of ancient Egypt and the enduring appeal of this goddess. These representations are not only valuable historical and cultural artifacts but also sources of inspiration and spiritual connection for people today.

Chapter 14: The Protective Goddess

Isis's role as a protector is a central theme in her mythology, symbolizing strength, care, and the safeguarding of the innocent and vulnerable. Her protective nature is particularly emphasized in her relationships with children, women, and the deceased, making her one of the most venerated deities in ancient Egyptian religion. This chapter explores Isis's protective aspects, her significance as a guardian deity, and the ways in which her protective nature was invoked and revered.

Isis as the Protector of Children

Isis's protective role was most poignantly expressed in her relationship with children. As the mother of Horus, she was depicted as the ideal mother figure, fiercely guarding her son against all threats, particularly from Set, the god of chaos and disorder. This maternal aspect made her a guardian deity for mothers and children across Egypt. Mothers would invoke Isis for the health and safety of their children, and amulets bearing her likeness were often used as talismans to safeguard the young.

Guardian of Women and Families

Isis was also seen as a protector of women, particularly in their roles as mothers and wives. Her own experiences of love, loss, and resilience resonated deeply with the women of ancient Egypt, who saw in her a divine advocate and guardian. She was invoked in matters of love, fertility, and domestic harmony, providing spiritual support and protection in the various challenges faced by women.

The Protector in the Afterlife

Another crucial aspect of Isis's protective role was in the afterlife. In funerary texts and rituals, Isis was often called upon to safeguard the deceased on their journey to the afterlife. She was believed to use her magical powers to ward off evil spirits and to guide the souls of the dead to safety. Her wings, often depicted in tomb paintings and sarcophagi, were symbols of her embracing protection, covering the deceased in a protective embrace.

The Magical Protector

Isis's prowess in magic was a key element of her protective nature. She was considered to be one of the most powerful magicians among the Egyptian gods, using her knowledge to protect those in need. Her magic was seen as a force of good, countering the chaos and destruction brought about by malevolent forces. This aspect of her character was particularly emphasized in tales where she used her magical skills to outwit more powerful foes, thereby protecting her family and followers.

Isis in the Community

The protective aspect of Isis was not limited to personal and familial domains but extended to the community and the kingdom. She was seen as a guardian of the pharaoh and, by extension, the entire land of Egypt. Her protection ensured the stability and prosperity of the kingdom, warding off natural disasters and external threats.

Meditation: Protective Shield Meditation for Safety and Security

In the spirit of Isis's protective nature, let us engage in a meditation to create a protective shield around ourselves, drawing inspiration from the goddess's strength and guardianship.

Find a quiet and comfortable place where you can sit or lie down. Close your eyes, and take a few deep breaths, allowing your body to relax. Visualize yourself in a serene space, a place where you feel safe and at peace.

In this space, imagine the presence of Isis, her figure radiating strength, warmth, and protection. Feel her protective energy surrounding you, forming a luminous shield around your body.

As you sit within this shield, visualize it being strengthened by the qualities of Isis – her courage, her wisdom, and her nurturing care. Imagine this shield guarding you against negativity, harm, and fear, allowing only positivity and love to enter your space.

Sit with this visualization for a few moments, feeling completely safe and secure within this protective shield. When you feel ready, gently bring yourself back to the present, carrying with you the sense of security and peace you have cultivated.

Isis's role as a protector in ancient Egyptian mythology provides a powerful archetype of guardianship, care, and magical prowess. Her protective nature, transcending the personal to the communal and the spiritual realms, offers a timeless model of strength and nurturing care. In modern times, her legacy continues to inspire and offer solace, reminding us of the enduring power of protection and care in our lives.

Chapter 15: Myths and Legends Surrounding Isis

The mythology surrounding Isis, one of the most significant and complex deities in ancient Egyptian religion, is rich with stories of magic, intrigue, love, and resilience. These myths not only provide insight into the religious and cultural practices of ancient Egypt but also offer timeless narratives of human experiences and emotions. This chapter delves into some of the most prominent and enduring myths and legends surrounding Isis, exploring the depth and breadth of her influence in the pantheon of Egyptian gods.

The Search for Osiris

One of the most famous myths involving Isis is the tale of her search for her husband, Osiris. After Osiris was betrayed and killed by his brother Set, who was jealous of his power, Isis embarked on a long and arduous journey to find his body. Her relentless search and deep love for Osiris are central themes in this story, highlighting her devotion, determination, and magical prowess.

Upon finding his body and bringing it back to Egypt, Isis used her magical abilities to resurrect Osiris, making it possible for her to conceive their son, Horus. However, Set discovered the body again and dismembered it, scattering the pieces across Egypt. Isis, undeterred, searched for each piece and, with the help of her sister Nephthys, Anubis, and other gods, reassembled Osiris's body and resurrected him once more. This time, Osiris became the ruler of the underworld, symbolizing the cycle of life, death, and rebirth.

The Birth of Horus

Another central myth in the Isis canon is the birth and upbringing of her son, Horus. Isis, knowing that Set would be a threat to her son, hid Horus in the marshes of the Nile Delta. There, she raised him in secret, protecting him from the dangers posed by Set.

One of the most well-known stories from Horus's childhood is when he was stung by a scorpion and fell gravely ill. In her grief and desperation, Isis cried out to the heavens for help. Her pleas were heard, and through the intervention of the god Thoth, Horus was healed. This myth underscores Isis's role as a protective mother and her magical skills in warding off danger and curing illness.

The Contendings of Horus and Set

The struggle between Horus and Set for the throne of Egypt is another significant myth involving Isis. This conflict, which lasted for eighty years, involved a series of battles and legal disputes before the gods. Isis, ever the strategic and cunning goddess, played a crucial role in these events, using her wisdom and magical abilities to aid her son.

In one notable episode, Isis transformed herself into a young maiden and tricked Set into making a statement that weakened his legal claim to the throne. Her intervention was pivotal in securing Horus's victory and the restoration of order and justice in Egypt.

Isis's Journey to Byblos

The myth of Isis's journey to Byblos showcases her determination and resourcefulness. In her search for Osiris's body, she traveled to Byblos, where she discovered that a pillar containing Osiris's body had been used in the construction of a palace. Disguising herself as an old woman, she gained the trust of the queen and became the nurse to her infant son.

To grant the infant immortality, Isis placed him in fire while she transformed into a swallow, circling the pillar containing Osiris's body. The queen, witnessing this, interrupted the ritual, thus preventing the child's immortality. However, moved by Isis's story and her quest to resurrect Osiris, the king of Byblos agreed to give her the pillar, aiding in her mission to revive her husband.

Meditation: Journey into the World of Myths

To connect with the rich mythology of Isis, engage in a journey meditation that transports you into the world of these ancient stories. Find a comfortable and quiet place to sit or lie down. Close your eyes, take deep breaths, and allow your body to relax.

Imagine yourself traveling back in time to ancient Egypt, to a world where gods and goddesses walk among the people. Visualize the lush banks of the Nile, the majestic pyramids, and the bustling cities.

See yourself witnessing the key events in the myths of Isis – her search for Osiris, the upbringing of Horus, and her clever strategies in the contendings against Set. Observe these stories as if you are there, feeling the emotions and the ambiance of each scene.

As you journey through these myths, reflect on the themes of love, resilience, wisdom, and justice. Contemplate how these stories resonate with your own life experiences and the lessons they offer. When you feel ready, gently bring yourself back to the present, carrying with you the insights and inspirations from this meditative journey.

The myths and legends surrounding Isis offer a rich tapestry of storytelling that continues to fascinate and inspire. These ancient narratives, filled with magic, intrigue, and profound emotion, not only reflect the religious beliefs of their time but also speak to universal human experiences that transcend time and culture.

Chapter 16: Comparative Mythology: Isis and Other Goddesses

The figure of Isis in Egyptian mythology is a rich tapestry of characteristics and narratives, many of which find echoes in the goddesses of other cultures and mythologies. This chapter explores these comparative mythological elements, drawing parallels between Isis and other divine feminine figures across various traditions. The aim is to illuminate the universal aspects of the goddess archetype and the way different cultures have shaped this concept.

Isis and Demeter (Greek Mythology)

One of the most direct comparisons can be made between Isis and Demeter of Greek mythology. Both are primarily seen as mother goddesses associated with agriculture and fertility. Demeter's grief over the abduction of her daughter Persephone by Hades bears a striking resemblance to Isis's grief for Osiris. Both goddesses' stories reflect the cycles of nature – death and rebirth – and their narratives are central to the agricultural myths of their respective cultures.

Isis and Mary (Christianity)

In Christian iconography and theology, the Virgin Mary shares several attributes with Isis, especially in her role as the mother of Jesus. Like Isis, Mary is often depicted in a protective role, with a strong emphasis on her maternal qualities. The iconic image of Isis holding the infant Horus is paralleled in the Christian portrayal of Mary holding the baby Jesus. Both figures embody the divine feminine's nurturing, compassionate aspects and have a significant following devoted to their worship.

Isis and Kali/Durga (Hindu Mythology)

In Hindu mythology, the goddesses Kali and Durga represent the powerful, assertive aspect of the divine feminine. While at first, they may seem quite different from the nurturing image of Isis, there are underlying similarities. Like Isis, Kali and Durga are often invoked for protection against evil and are revered as powerful mother figures. Their narratives also encompass themes of creation, destruction, and rebirth, much like the story of Isis and Osiris.

Isis and Inanna/Ishtar (Mesopotamian Mythology)

Inanna (or Ishtar, in the Akkadian tradition) was a prominent goddess in Mesopotamian mythology, associated with love, beauty, sex, war, justice, and political power. Like Isis, Inanna embarked on an epic journey – her descent into the underworld – which has parallels with Isis's search for Osiris. Both goddesses display a blend of vulnerability and strength, and their myths encompass the themes of love, loss, and resurrection.

Isis and Freyja (Norse Mythology)

Freyja, a major goddess in Norse mythology, shares several attributes with Isis. Both are associated with love, beauty, and fertility. Freyja, like Isis, is a multifaceted goddess who commands magic and is capable of fierce protection and deep compassion. The way these goddesses are revered in their respective cultures highlights the universal aspects of the divine feminine as both nurturing and powerful.

Meditation: Unity Meditation on the Divine Feminine

To connect with the universal aspects of the divine feminine embodied by Isis and other goddesses, let us engage in a unity meditation.

Find a comfortable and quiet place where you can sit or lie down undisturbed. Close your eyes and take deep, slow breaths to center yourself.

Visualize a serene and beautiful garden, a symbolic meeting place of different goddesses from various cultures. In this garden, see figures of Isis, Demeter, Mary, Kali, Inanna, and Freyja, each embodying different aspects of the divine feminine.

As you observe these goddesses, reflect on the qualities they share – their strength, wisdom, nurturing care, and their connection to the cycles of nature and life. Contemplate the universal aspects of the divine feminine, recognizing how these deities, despite their cultural differences, represent common themes and experiences.

Feel a sense of unity and connection with these goddesses, understanding that they symbolize the shared human experience and the collective unconscious. Allow yourself to be filled with a sense of peace, empowerment, and oneness with the divine feminine.

When you feel ready, gently bring yourself back to the present, carrying with you a sense of connection and unity with the divine feminine across different cultures and mythologies.

The comparative mythology of Isis and other goddesses highlights the universal themes and attributes of the divine feminine. These narratives, spanning different cultures and eras, reflect the shared human experience and the enduring power of the goddess archetype in human consciousness.

Chapter 17: The Legacy of Isis

The figure of Isis, one of the most complex and enduring deities of ancient Egyptian mythology, has left an indelible mark on various aspects of culture, religion, and esoteric traditions. Her legacy extends far beyond the ancient world, influencing art, literature, spiritual practices, and even political ideologies. This chapter explores the multifaceted impact of Isis throughout history and into the modern era, highlighting how her image and mythology have been adapted and reinterpreted over the centuries.

Isis in the Greco-Roman World

The influence of Isis began to spread beyond Egypt during the Hellenistic period, particularly after Egypt became a province of the Roman Empire. In the Greco-Roman world, Isis was syncretized with Greek and Roman goddesses such as Demeter, Artemis, and Venus. Her cult became one of the most popular in the Roman Empire, with temples dedicated to her from Britain to Afghanistan. The universal appeal of Isis in the Greco-Roman world laid the groundwork for her enduring influence in Western culture.

Isis in Art and Literature

The image of Isis has been a source of inspiration in various forms of art and literature throughout history. In Renaissance art, she was often depicted in the guise of the Madonna, reflecting the blending of pagan and Christian iconography. In literature, her story has been retold and reimagined in countless ways, from Shakespeare's references to her in "Antony and Cleopatra" to her role in contemporary novels and poetry. Her image as a powerful and compassionate deity continues to resonate with artists and writers.

Isis in Esoteric and Occult Traditions

In the 19th and 20th centuries, the figure of Isis experienced a resurgence in esoteric and occult circles. She became a central figure in various mystical traditions, such as Theosophy and the Hermetic Order of the Golden Dawn. In these traditions, Isis symbolizes the mysteries of the divine feminine, magic, and spiritual initiation. Her mythology is often interpreted allegorically, representing the journey of the soul towards enlightenment.

The Modern Spiritual Movement

In contemporary spiritual movements, particularly those focusing on the divine feminine, Isis holds a place of honor. She is seen as a goddess of empowerment, healing, and spiritual wisdom. Modern devotees draw inspiration from her strength, resilience, and deep knowledge. The adaptability of her myth to various spiritual paths and interpretations underlines her continued relevance.

Political and Cultural Symbolism

The legacy of Isis has also been adopted in political and cultural symbolism. For instance, the image of the goddess holding Horus has influenced representations of motherhood and royalty. In a broader sense, Isis has come to represent the enduring nature of Egyptian culture and its influence on the world.

Meditation: Contemplating Our Legacy

In light of the enduring legacy of Isis, let's engage in a meditation that focuses on contemplating our own impact on the world. Find a quiet place to sit comfortably. Close your eyes, take deep breaths, and allow your body to relax.

Imagine yourself in a peaceful setting, a place that gives you a sense of tranquility and perspective. Reflect on the legacy of Isis, her journey through history, and the many lives she has touched.

Now, turn your thoughts inward. Contemplate your life and the impact you have had on the people around you. Think about the roles you play, your actions, and your words. How have they influenced others? What positive changes have you brought to your community?

Consider the legacy you wish to leave behind. How do you want to be remembered? What contributions do you want to make to the world? Visualize yourself making these contributions, however big or small, and the ripple effects they create.

Take a few moments to sit with these thoughts, feeling a sense of purpose and connection with the broader tapestry of life. When you feel ready, gently bring yourself back to the present, carrying with you the insights and inspiration from this meditation.

The legacy of Isis, transcending time and culture, serves as a powerful reminder of the enduring impact of myth, religion, and cultural symbols on human history. Her story, evolving and adapting through centuries, continues to inspire and influence, reminding us of the potential for enduring influence and the power of legacy in our lives.

Chapter 18: Isis and Alchemy

Alchemy, the ancient art and science of transformation, has long been shrouded in mystery and symbolism. Within its rich tapestry of metaphors and allegories, the figure of Isis occupies a significant place, symbolizing transformation, regeneration, and the mysteries of the universe. This chapter explores the role of Isis in alchemical texts and symbolism, her connection to alchemical processes, and how these ancient practices relate to modern concepts of personal and spiritual transformation.

Isis in Alchemical Tradition

In alchemical tradition, Isis is often portrayed as the archetypal sorceress, a master of the hidden arts, and the keeper of secret knowledge. She is sometimes equated with nature itself, embodying the principle of transformation that is at the heart of alchemical practice. Her search for and reassembly of Osiris's body is seen as an allegory for the alchemical process of separating and recombining substances to achieve a higher state of being.

The Symbolism of the Veil

One of the most potent symbols associated with Isis in alchemy is the veil. In one of her most famous sayings, Isis declares, "I am all that has been, that is, and that will be, and no mortal has yet dared to lift my veil." In alchemy, this veil represents the mysteries of nature and the secrets of the material world. The alchemist's quest is often depicted as an attempt to lift this veil, to understand and harness the hidden forces of nature.

The Alchemical Marriage

Isis also plays a role in the concept of the 'alchemical marriage,' a key theme in alchemical symbolism. This is the union of opposing elements or principles, often represented by the sun (masculine) and the moon (feminine). Isis, in her role as the divine feminine, symbolizes one half of this cosmic union. Her reunion with Osiris can be interpreted as an allegorical representation of this alchemical marriage, symbolizing the unification and harmonization of dualities.

Isis and the Philosopher's Stone

In some alchemical texts, Isis is closely associated with the quest for the Philosopher's Stone, the legendary substance capable of turning base metals into gold and granting immortality. This quest is symbolic of the search for spiritual enlightenment and the transformation of the soul. Isis, as a guide and a symbol of divine wisdom, represents both the journey and the ultimate goal of this spiritual alchemy.

Modern Interpretations of Alchemical Isis

In modern psychology, particularly in the work of Carl Jung, alchemical symbols, including those associated with Isis, are interpreted as representations of processes in the unconscious mind. Jung saw the figure of Isis as embodying the anima, the feminine aspect of the male psyche, and a symbol of the transformative power of the subconscious.

Meditation: Personal Alchemy Transformation

Inspired by the alchemical symbolism of Isis, engage in a meditation focused on personal transformation and spiritual alchemy.

Find a quiet and comfortable place to sit. Close your eyes and take several deep breaths, allowing yourself to relax. Visualize yourself in an ancient alchemical laboratory, surrounded by books, herbs, and alchemical instruments.

In this sacred space, envision the presence of Isis, guiding you in your alchemical work. See yourself working with the basic elements of your life – your challenges, fears, hopes, and dreams. Imagine yourself combining these elements in a symbolic alchemical process, guided by the wisdom of Isis.

As you engage in this inner alchemy, envision a transformation taking place within you. See yourself turning your base experiences, your struggles and pains, into spiritual gold – wisdom, strength, and inner peace.

Feel a sense of empowerment and renewal as you undergo this transformation. When you feel ready, gently bring yourself back to the present, carrying with you the insights and growth from your alchemical journey.

The role of Isis in alchemy serves as a powerful metaphor for transformation and enlightenment, both in the material and spiritual realms. Her enduring legacy in this mystical tradition continues to inspire those on a path of personal and spiritual growth, reminding us of the transformative power within each of us.

Chapter 19: Isis in Literature and Popular Culture

The mythological figure of Isis has transcended time and culture, continually being reimagined and reinterpreted in modern literature, movies, and media. Her character, rich in symbolism and depth, offers a wellspring of inspiration for contemporary storytellers and artists. This chapter delves into the portrayal of Isis in various modern artistic mediums, exploring how this ancient deity continues to captivate and influence the modern imagination.

Isis in Modern Literature

In modern literature, Isis often appears as a symbol of power, mystery, and the divine feminine. Authors have reimagined her story in various genres, from historical fiction to fantasy. In these narratives, she is sometimes depicted in her traditional mythological form, while other times she is reinterpreted, embodying contemporary themes of empowerment, spirituality, and transformation.

Notable examples include novels where Isis's mythology is woven into the plot, providing a backdrop for stories of love, intrigue, and spiritual awakening. Poets have also found inspiration in Isis, using her as a metaphor for nature's cycles, the mysteries of womanhood, or the quest for knowledge and enlightenment.

Isis in Film and Television

In the realm of film and television, Isis has been portrayed in both literal and symbolic ways. She often appears in historical dramas and documentaries about ancient Egypt, depicted according to traditional iconography and mythological narratives.

In fantasy and science fiction, filmmakers have reimagined Isis, sometimes placing her in contemporary settings or alternate worlds. These portrayals often emphasize her aspects as a powerful sorceress or a wise guide, resonating with modern audiences' fascination with supernatural and mystical themes.

Isis in Comics and Graphic Novels

Isis has also made her mark in the world of comics and graphic novels. In this medium, her character is often reenvisioned as a superhero or a mystical entity, blending ancient mythology with modern superhero tropes. These stories typically focus on themes of justice, power, and the use of supernatural abilities for the greater good.

Isis in Music and Performance Art

Musicians and performance artists have also drawn inspiration from Isis, using her image and story to explore themes of femininity, strength, and transformation. In music, references to Isis can be found in songs' lyrics and in the personas adopted by performers. In dance and performance art, her myth has been interpreted through various forms, from classical ballet to modern interpretive dance, often highlighting her story's emotional and symbolic depth.

Isis in Video Games and Digital Media

In the realm of video games and digital media, Isis often appears in titles that draw on mythological and historical themes. In these games, she can be a character to interact with or even a playable character, allowing players to experience aspects of her mythology in an interactive format.

Meditation: Creative Expression Inspired by Modern Interpretations

In the spirit of the modern interpretations of Isis, engage in a meditation focused on creative expression, drawing inspiration from the diverse portrayals of this ancient goddess.

Find a comfortable and quiet place to sit or lie down. Close your eyes and take deep breaths, allowing your body and mind to relax.

Visualize a blank canvas or an empty stage in front of you, representing your own creative potential. Imagine Isis beside you, in whatever form resonates with you – be it a traditional depiction or a modern reinterpretation.

As you sit with the presence of Isis, allow her essence to inspire you. Think about the ways you can express her qualities – strength, wisdom, creativity – in your own life and work. Whether through writing, art, music, or any other form of expression, envision yourself channeling the spirit of Isis into your creations.

Allow this meditation to be a free space for your imagination. There are no boundaries or limitations – just the flow of inspiration from the figure of Isis into your own creative expression.

When you feel ready, gently bring yourself back to the present, carrying with you the inspiration and energy from this meditative experience.

The portrayal of Isis in modern literature, movies, and media reflects her enduring appeal and the versatility of her myth. As a character and symbol, she continues to inspire, challenge, and captivate, demonstrating the timeless power of myth and the ongoing relevance of ancient deities in contemporary culture.

Chapter 20: Embodying the Wisdom of Isis

The ancient figure of Isis, with her multifaceted roles as a goddess of magic, motherhood, and wisdom, offers profound insights for modern living. Embodying her wisdom in daily life involves integrating her qualities of compassion, resilience, intelligence, and balance into our personal and professional spheres. This chapter explores practical ways to incorporate the teachings and qualities of Isis into everyday life, along with a meditation practice to deepen this integration.

Embracing Resilience and Adaptability

One of the most striking aspects of Isis is her resilience. Faced with the murder and dismemberment of her husband Osiris, she tirelessly sought to bring him back to life. Embodying Isis's resilience means cultivating the ability to overcome challenges and setbacks in our own lives. It involves maintaining hope and determination in the face of adversity, and being adaptable when confronted with change.

Nurturing Compassion and Empathy

Isis's role as a nurturing mother to Horus and her compassion towards humanity are central to her mythology. To embody these qualities, we can strive to cultivate empathy and understanding in our relationships. This involves actively listening to others, offering support and kindness, and practicing patience and tolerance in our daily interactions.

Balancing Wisdom and Power

As a goddess of wisdom, Isis was revered for her deep knowledge and sound judgment. Embodying this aspect involves cultivating a balanced perspective in life, making decisions not just based on logic or emotion, but a harmonious blend of both. It also means using our power and influence responsibly, aiming to benefit the greater good rather than purely personal interests.

Cultivating Magical and Spiritual Awareness

Isis's mastery of magic symbolizes the power of transformation and the unseen forces that shape our lives. To embody this, we can engage in practices that heighten our spiritual awareness, such as meditation, mindfulness, and self-reflection. These practices help us connect with our inner wisdom and the subtle energies that influence our being and surroundings.

Seeking Knowledge and Personal Growth

Isis's quest for the pieces of Osiris can be seen as a metaphor for the pursuit of knowledge and wholeness. Embodying this quality involves a commitment to lifelong learning and personal development. It means being open to new experiences, ideas, and perspectives, and actively seeking opportunities for growth and self-improvement.

Meditation: Integrative Meditation for Wisdom and Guidance

To integrate the wisdom and guidance of Isis into our lives, let's practice an integrative meditation.

Find a quiet place where you can sit comfortably without being disturbed. Close your eyes, and take deep, slow breaths to relax your mind and body.

Visualize yourself in a serene setting, perhaps beside the Nile or in an ancient Egyptian temple. Feel the presence of Isis with you, her figure embodying strength, compassion, and wisdom.

In this sacred space, reflect on the qualities of Isis you wish to embody. Whether it's her resilience, empathy, wisdom, spiritual awareness, or her thirst for knowledge, visualize these qualities merging with your own energy field.

Imagine these qualities as beams of light, entering your body and mind, illuminating you from within. Feel yourself absorbing these attributes, becoming more resilient, compassionate, wise, spiritually aware, and open to learning.

As you bask in this integration, ask Isis for guidance or clarity on any issue you're facing.

Listen with your heart for any insights or intuitions that may arise.

When you feel the meditation is complete, gently bring your awareness back to the present moment. Open your eyes, carrying with you the wisdom and guidance of Isis into your daily life.

Embodying the wisdom of Isis in our modern lives means integrating her enduring qualities into our everyday actions and decisions. By doing so, we honor the legacy of this ancient goddess and enrich our own lives with her timeless virtues.

Printed in Great Britain
by Amazon